Yes, You Can

A Guide to Writing and Sharing Your Story

Isabella D. Morganthal

Yes, You Can: A Guide to Writing and Sharing Your Story

Copyright © April 2017 by Isabella Drew Morganthal
All Rights Reserved
Printed in the United States of America

This book is protected under copyright and needs written permission from the author before any information is copied. *Thank you.*

Scriptures taken from the Holy Bible, New King James Version®, NKJV®. Copyright© 1973, 1978, 1984 by Biblica, Inc. ™ Used by permission of Zondervan. All rights reserved worldwide.

This book is in no way endorsed or sponsored by CreateSpace, Amazon, or their affiliates.

Published by Morganthal Press
thekingsprincessmagazine@gmail.com
Cover design by Isabella Morganthal and BushMaid Design
ISBN # 1545018219

*All I have is because of Jesus, for Jesus,
and in Jesus.
Father, it's for You.
You have all my love.*

Where to Find It

A Note for You...................09
Writing.........................15
Editing.........................33
Publishing......................43
Sharing.........................51
Story Prompts...................61
Writing Exercises...............67
A Word about Dreams.............73
Thank You.......................77
Contact.........................78

A Note for You

It was a simple creative writing assignment that started it all.

If you would've told my eight-year-old self that day how all this would turn out, I would never have believed you.

I was homeschooled the whole way through to graduation, a blessing that I wish more people in this world could have.

Far from the unsocialized homeschooler that this world ridiculously portrays, I was an energetic, talkative, eight-year-old with a world of characters inside of her head that needed their story to be told on paper.

Then one day for school my mom (moms seriously make the best teachers) gave my twin sister and I a creative writing assignment.

And that day started it all.

I began by writing a short story (to me it was a "book") about a girl named Jenna and her black horse, Midnight. While completing this assignment, it was like a lightbulb went off in my head. A lightbulb moment that would only become clearer as I got older.

This was what I was meant to do.

This is what God's dream was for me.

I fell in love.

Writing became my love, my passion, my joy. Writing was basically my life. Still is.

I continued my story about Jenna and Midnight and filled notebooks with all of their adventures. Next I moved onto a story about a little girl and her best friend, in my longest story at that point, *Best Friends Forever*.

When I got to the story of Mel and her Pinto, Chess, in my first real book, *Storm*, I had fallen head over heels in love with writing fiction. The characters and the world inside of my head were almost real to me. (Don't get freaked out just yet. I get weirder than that, trust me.)

I wrote every chance I had. And I read. I read every book I could get my hands on. Because here's a secret.

The best way to learn to write is to read.

My stories turned into novels. My characters fought bigger battles than the ones Jenna and Midnight had fought. I grew older and as I did I began writing about real life problems and characters who faced them.

I'm nineteen years old as I pen these words, and I've written nine fiction books or novels. I've also written four non-fiction books/devotionals, three of which are published.

Yes, I had discovered another love of mine.

The love of sharing my heart on paper in a more real way than I did with fiction.

When I wrote articles, non-fiction, or devotionals, I was pouring my heart and soul onto a paper and sharing a piece of *my* world. This piece of my world was different than my characters' world.

And I adored it.

My first book, *I Dare You: Finding Your Passion and Lighting Your World* released on June 26, 2015. *The King's Princess: A Magazine Compilation* released next on April 28, 2016. My third book, *Worth it All: Running the Race of a Lifetime* released not long after on October 30, 2016.

When I write I know this is what I was made to do. God created me to speak through my fingertips and share a story with the world that only He could write in my heart.

You too?

Well, friend, you've come to the right place.

This is for the dreamers, the writers, the ones with characters inside their mind aching to get on that paper. It's to the one with a message God is asking them to share, the one with a story on their heart aching to be told. *This is for you.* The writer who isn't sure how to start writing and the writer who has written for years but isn't sure where to go from there.

This little guide is my way of stepping into a piece of your journey to take you by the hand and encourage you to keep going.

Because I know.

I know writing can be hard.

Oh, I know.

So while this book is like your how-to-guide to writing and publishing from my perspective, it's also me looking into those beautiful, bright eyes of yours and whispering...

Yes, you can.

You can do this.
I believe in you. God believes in you.
And now you must believe in you too.
Ready?
Pick up your pen.
It's time to write.

"And let us not grow weary while doing good, for in due season we shall reap if we do not lose heart."

~Galatians 6:9~

Writing

I've been writing for over ten years and, by the grace of God, I'm the published author of three books.

I have young writers ask me all the time about writing, asking me for tips, or encouragement. I have seasoned writers asking me all the time about publishing and how to go about it.

That's why this guide was created, because I want to help you on your writing journey to reach for the stars, and pursue God's purpose for your writing.

But to walk this journey, you have to just *write*.

Sounds easy enough, right?

Wrong.

Trust me, I know. It's anything but easy. Simple, maybe. Easy? *No.*

Starting to write is maybe one of the hardest parts of the writing journey.

Even if you know exactly what you want to say, it's so hard to just begin. Beginning is everything. And we feel it has to be perfect.

Well, here's the first thing I want to tell you.

Perfect is overrated.

Perfect? Nah

If you're waiting for perfection to write or begin your story, I have news for you.

You'll never write.

Because, friend, here's the truth.

No one is perfect.

No writer is perfect. Not even that author you've been reading since you were a kid and all of your favorite books come from her/him. They're not perfect either. And I would also go as far as to say that their early writings might not have been the most entertaining read ever.

Writing is a process. A learning process.

And achieving perfection isn't a part of that process. Your writing will never be perfect.

It doesn't have to be.

God uses the broken things of this world to reveal beauty and He uses the weak things to show His strength.

So believe me when I tell you that I know He can use your imperfection to do something pretty amazing.

Looking back on my first published book, *I Dare You*, I cringe at parts where I don't think it was really that good. I cringe at parts that I think could've been better—*could've been more perfect.*

But guess what?

God has used this book to change lives *just the way it is.* I've heard from so many people, even people I do not know, who have told me that this book changed their lives. And I know it's because this book belongs to God first. It's *His.* So because of that, He can use it completely, imperfections and all.

He can do the same for you.

So don't let perfection hold you back or you'll be holding back forever.

Figure Out Your Style

What do you want to write most of all? What writing makes you happiest?

Maybe you love the fiction world inside of your head where you can create short stories, books, novels. Maybe you're a bit obsessed with the feelings that poetry, lyrics, or quotes create.

Maybe articles, devotionals, or non-fiction is more your thing.

Whatever you love to write the most, write that.

But don't settle with that.

That's right; I'm telling you to get out of your comfort zone. ☺

I've written fiction for as long as I could remember. Fiction was my love and I was comfortable with it. It made sense to me.

Writing non-fiction seemed too vulnerable to me at first. Too uncomfortable. It was something that placed my heart in front of the world in a new and different way that seemed terrifying.

But you know what?

If I had never stepped out of my comfort zone into the seemingly scary place of writing non-fiction, I never would've discovered my deepest passion. I never would've discovered what God had in store for my future.

So this is what I challenge you.

Whatever you love to write most, make sure you write that and write lots of it. But also figure out what scares you the most. Figure out what kind of writing makes you most uncomfortable. Then write that too.

A good writer writes anything. So write anything and everything. Write novels, devotionals, essays, and poems on the side. Write it all.

Somewhere along the way you'll discover what exactly you were created to write.

Just Do It

Yep, it's as simple as that.

It's as simple as three words. **Just. Do. It.**

Just write.

Wear Nike shoes if you have to, to help you remember. Write sticky notes on your mirror reminding you to "*Write today!!!*" Put reminders on your phone or computer.

I don't care what you have to do, but always remember to just write.

Writing is what makes you a writer. So write. Every day. Every chance you get. Whether it's good or not. You can always edit later.

So pick up your pen.

Yes, right now. Pick up your pen and go write something. Write for ten minutes. I don't care if all you write is, "*Someday I want to be published.*" Just write it. Write out your dreams if you want to. Write whatever. But go do that right now.

Here are some things that helped me get started with just writing...

Read. Trust me, reading is where you are going to learn the most. So read, read, and read some more. There's an endless supply of awesome books out there to read, so go pick some up at the library and start devouring them. (Note: I encourage you to read what's edifying and encouraging, even in fiction, and to stay away from anything that could keep you back from God's best for you. Ask your parents for help with finding books that will be good for you.) The authors whose books I've read have influenced and impacted my writing in ways that I never could've imagined. I think I must have been born with a book in my hand because I've been reading for as long as I can remember. Reading is how I learned a lot of how to format and edit my own books. Reading is how I learned better how to communicate my message. The great authors out there who have influenced and inspired me in writing are Ann Voskamp, Holley Gerth, Bob Goff, Lacey Sturm, Martha Finley, Tiffany Schlichter, Dannah Gresh, and MacKenzie Morganthal (yep, my twin). I would highly recommend their books to anyone.

So read. The next book you read may be the inspiration you need to write the next New York Times Bestseller.

Keep a journal. Ah, yes, I've been doing this for also as long as I can remember. Pretty much since I could hold a pen and write. Ask my mom. I have "journals" from when I was like five and six. Not exactly something I'd share with the world someday, but hey it got me started. Keeping a journal has been like a safe haven for me. A place where I can go and express my feelings, my thoughts. A place where I can go and talk to God. I've always talked best through my fingers (although I still talk too much with my mouth too), so keeping a journal was usually how I prayed best. Especially during my teenage years, journaling was one of my favorite things to do. Your personal journal is between you and God so you have the freedom to write your heart out to Him. Journal as much as you can, every day if possible. I used to journal every day as a little girl, but of course that changed when I got busy as a young adult. Journaling exercises your writing muscle, so use it lots!

Use writing exercises/prompts. These are seriously so fun. ☺ I have a few for you in the back of this book that I've created but there is a giant resource of them out there. There are tons of places online with writing exercises or prompts and there are even books created especially for this. I had a book of writing exercises when I was younger and it was awesome! Oh, and there's Pinterest too. Raise your hand if you're a Pinterest addict like me (You might as well admit it). Pinterest is incredible for writing prompts. Of course, with anything, you need to be careful, so for younger readers, definitely check with your parents before using. But seriously, Pinterest has helped me overcome writer's block so many times.

However you have to do it, whatever helps best, just make sure you're writing. It only gets easier from here.

A Word about Writer's Block

Oh, yes, the dreaded term for any writer.

Writer's block.

Enter the sick feeling, the eye roll, and the heart racing.

Okay, maybe you're not as dramatic as me.

Anyway, every writer knows how dreaded writer's block is. And oddly, it eventually happens to every writer.

Never dealt with it?

Well, enjoy it while it lasts. But get prepared for it to come.

Writer's block is like the writer's version of walking through a desert for who knows how long without any supply of water.

Told you I'm dramatic.

But it feels like the truth, doesn't it? If you're a dramatic writer like me you know exactly what I'm talking about.

Writer's block is hard. It's when you sit down at the computer and the story in your heart is bubbling to get out but you just have absolutely no idea how to get it out. It's when you sit down at your computer and you literally have no ideas, no words, no *nothing*.

It can be so hard to get out of. It can be hard to come out of this dry spell and get back into the habit of writing.

I'm no expert at this, trust me. And writer's block hits me a lot more than I would like it to.

But here's something I've learned through the deserts of writer's block.

It's kind of like a unicorn.

Don't get all weirded out on me yet. And also, please don't throw this book away. Because I do have an explanation.

A unicorn is a figment of someone's imagination. It's not reality. It's not real. It's only what they've created in their mind.

Same with writer's block.

It's in your mind. It's not real.

Yes, I know it can feel like you have no inspiration or you have no idea how to write what you want to next. I know it can feel impossible.

But stop convincing yourself that writer's block is real. Because convincing yourself of that only gives it more power in your life.

Convince yourself that *you can* write. Because yes, *you can*!

And then write. Write through the desert.

Even if it's the worst thing you've ever written, write it anyway.

The only way to conquer writer's block is to write as if it doesn't exist.

Pray

A secret about my books? *They're not actually mine.*

You see, from the moment I sit down at the computer, open up Microsoft Word (my favorite place to be), and begin typing a new title across the blank page, I dedicate the words.

Every single word I type does not belong to me. I dedicate every sentence, every chapter, every book to God. I pray hard over every book I write and I pray over the books I sign to readers.

Sitting down at my computer to work on a book, I pray the same thing every time.

Father, write through me today.

Speak through me, speak Your words. Share Your truth. Let this story be Yours.

Honestly, words change lives.

The words we speak, the words we say, the words we read, they all affect us in some way.

And maybe that's why books are so powerful. Because words are powerful. Words can bring death or life.

When you write, whatever genre you are writing, you must ask yourself...

Why *am I writing?*

Why am I writing this story? Why am I sharing this tale? Why am I penning these words?

If you're writing for anything or anyone other than God, it will be pointless.

I will be perfectly honest with you when I say that. Whether you're writing a novel or a devotional, your words will be meaningless if you do not first give them to God.

Only God can make a thing great. Only God can use your words to change the world. Only God can use your story to inspire a generation. Only God can use your tale to impact lives.

So before anything else, you pray over those words.

Friend, you pray hard.

Because here's another secret.

When you are writing for God and for His glory, your writing is being thrown into the midst of a battle.

Your writing will become a part of a war.

Our enemy wants to fight against these words God has given you. Our enemy wants to do anything to stop you from sharing your story. Because he knows that God can and will use your book or your story to change a life. And he doesn't want that to happen, so he's gonna fight you.

Makes you think differently about writer's block now, doesn't it?

Let me tell you a little story.

Although I've faced some form of spiritual warfare with each of the books I have written, mostly in the form of writer's block, I have felt it most strongly with two of my books. One published and one not even yet finished. (Y'all can keep a secret, right?)

The devil tried his best to keep me from writing my first published book, *I Dare You*. And he fought against me hard. Writer's block was intense. But I wrote anyway. So he attacked my thoughts. I was plagued with the idea that my writing was *not good enough*. That what I had to share with the world was below average, just not enough.

You too?

Good, then listen closely.

You are enough.

Your writing is *enough*.

Not because of you. But because when you give your writing into the hands of God, it becomes *His*. And He is so much more than enough. In Him, He makes you and your writing more than enough too. Trust me.

The devil didn't get his way with that book, so he's trying again. Right now I'm working on my next book to publish, a book with a message that I believe so strongly in and I know that God has a strong purpose for this book.

I have faced so much physical sickness during the writing of this book that has kept me from writing. I have faced severe headaches, stomach pain, and lots of fatigue.

I know in my heart this is because my book is in the middle of a battle.

Yours is too, my friend.

Yours is too because if you have given it to God, He is doing something amazing with it already.

But the good news?

Christ is victorious in you. So because of that *you are victorious* in this battle.

But you must fight. And you must fight hard.

Fight with prayer. Fight by writing. Fight with Scripture. Fight with the truth God has given you to defeat the lies attacking you.

I can't express enough how important it is to cover your book and your writing project in prayer.

Gather a group of trusted friends, mentors, or leaders to be your prayer warriors. They can come alongside you and cover you in prayer as you fight this battle of sharing the story God has given you with the world.

Also, don't think this is just for non-fiction writers or writers who are sharing a message or story that isn't fiction. Because fiction can be just as powerful. Ask my sister. Read her book actually. Fiction is powerful too and can be used by God in mighty ways. So you'll face this with fiction too.

Fight back with God.

Fight this war with prayer.

And write.

Press on to the End

A common problem with writing is that once we get over the difficulty of just beginning and we get through the rough middle, we tend to give up. Because finishing is hard too. Sometimes harder than we think it'll be.

So we move onto the next project and the next project, thinking it'll be easier with that one.

But it won't.

Finishing will always be hard. Pushing on until the end will seem like too much. Changing projects won't change that.

It's kind of funny I'm writing about that right now when I'm supposed to be writing my next book and I've gotten distracted by writing this booklet. But, hey, I want to share this with you all soon! ☺ (Good excuse, right?)

Here's my challenge to you.

Finish what you've started.

I love this verse from Galatians 6:9 that says:

"And let us not grow weary while doing good, for in due season we shall reap if we do not lose heart."

Don't grow weary, dear writer.

Keep on writing on.

Do not lose heart. Write until the end. Push to the finish line. I don't think there's any feeling in this world like the feeling after typing "THE END" onto the last page of a novel, or typing the final message into a devotional.

When you get to the end, it'll be worth it, I promise. It'll be worth the stress. It'll be worth the tears. It'll be worth the work. Because, yes, writing is a lot of work.

But if you press on until the end, *I know it's going to be worth it.*

Write until you run out of words to write. And when you've finished, get ready for the next step.

Because sometimes sharing your words is the hardest step of all.

Editing

I'll just give you a heads up for this section that I'm not an English major or anything. Editing isn't really my thing.

Yet I've edited all of my books, so I'm proof that you don't have to be an English major to learn how to edit.

We've already covered the fact that writing is not about perfectionism, so let's be clear that editing isn't about perfectionism either.

You don't have to have a college degree to know how to write and you don't have to have a college degree to know how to edit.

I know, so contrary to what the world and most people will tell you, but it's the truth. Just ask me. I'm the published author of three books, by God's grace, and didn't do college a day in my life.

So what's the big deal about editing? How do you go about editing? *And what's editing even mean?*

Well, let's go!

Read, Read, Read Again

You know that saying that goes, "if at first you don't succeed, try, try, try again"?

Well, I like to change that to, "after your first draft, read, read, read again."

Because that's the first step to editing your project. Read it like a million times.

Editing is the step of book writing that I like the least. When I was in the editing process of my book, *I Dare You*, I must have read it a couple dozen times (okay, more like forty or fifty times). I did all of the editing on my own for my first two books. Although this worked for me, I do recommend having help. When I was editing my third book, *Worth it All*, one of my dear friends, Dani, edited it too. Her input, advice, and grammar fixes were an abundance of help and I was super thankful for her.

Get a close friend, a sibling, a parent, someone you can trust, and ask them to help you edit. Even if they don't know anything about grammar they can still help you edit by seeing which parts are good and which parts can be left out or fixed.

My one advice is to be careful who you make your editing team and how many people you invite into your editing team.

Everyone has their own opinions and everyone will have different opinions. You can't possibly please everyone. So make sure your editing team is just two, three, or four close people you can trust for advice and go with that!

Then you read your manuscript and let them read your manuscript.

Over and over and over again. ☺

Each time you read look for something different or read it from a different perspective. Put yourself in the reader's shoes.

When reading, here are some important things to check for:

- o *Grammar, spelling.* Make sure words are spelled correctly and sentences are worded properly. It doesn't have to be perfect, but strive for excellence. Check for any mistakes you may have made in the rush of writing.

o *Sentence flow.* Make sure all your sentences flow smoothly and sound right. If you're unsure about how something sounds, ask a friend to read it and help you out!

o *Bible verses are accurate.* Make sure of this; it's important! Check to make sure the verses you include (if you include Scripture), are accurate with no mistakes and that they match the reference you wrote down. There were plenty of times in my books where I wrote the wrong reference number accidentally and caught it while editing.

o *Check quotes/excerpts for accuracy.* Do you quote someone in your book or include an excerpt from another book (with permission)? Do you have a notes or bibliography in the back for this? What about stating facts that you back up with a reference? Check to make sure anything you quote, excerpt from, or state as fact is true and written accurately. Also double check in your notes/bibliography that all of that information is accurate.

o *Page numbers.* I'm going to talk more about page numbers and formatting in a little bit, but when you're reading through your book, double check these too. Make sure all the page numbers are added in correctly and in the right places. With my book *Worth it All*, I missed a page number problem and didn't catch it until I had moved into the publishing stage and it almost delayed production. So double check this when editing!

I know that reading your book so many times can get overwhelming and even kind of boring, but trust me, it'll make things a lot easier in the end! So this is a super important step.

Formatting

After my book was written, edited, and read a couple dozen times, I began to format.

This was the stage of book publishing where I was close to giving up and I cried a lot. I had no idea what I was doing and I struggled with figuring out exactly *how* to format.

Because I don't want you to spend your time crying over formatting either, I'm here to offer you hope. *It's not really as bad as it seems. It can be done.* And I believe in you. I know you'll figure it out.

Since each program for writing is different, I can't really give specific directions on how to format or do page numbers because your program may be completely different from mine.

If you have specific questions on how to do page numbers or formatting (using Microsoft Word), I would be happy to answer your questions and help. You can find my contact information at the end of this book.

Every book needs page numbers. It's how readers find their favorite page or find a page they're looking for. So including page numbers is just about necessary! It makes editing easier for you too when the book is printed and you're editing from a printed proof.

A tip about page numbers: Leave them off of pages such as blank pages, title/copyright pages, or chapter title pages (if you have specific pages just with the title of each chapter on them).

You can do lots of fun things with page numbers and put them at the top or bottom of a page! All of my page numbers are on the bottom of my pages, but have fun with it experimenting and putting them where you want!

Some books, if you notice, include a header at the top of each page with either the book title, chapter title, or author name. This is optional. I didn't include this in my books just because of all the extra work involved, but if you want to include it, go for it! It can totally be done, it'll just take more time. Have fun experimenting with this too. I know it may seem like a lot of work, but book writing/publishing is seriously about doing what you love. So enjoy it!

Make sure to leave blank pages where they're necessary and to include a title and copyright page at the beginning of your manuscript.

I learned so much about formatting and what a book should look like by looking at the other books I've read, specifically other self-published books like mine. If you're having trouble figuring out where things should go or how your formatting should look, feel free to take a look at one of my books for ideas.

Above all, remember that your book is unique. So your formatting can be unique too. Design it how you want! Have fun including special designs and such! You need to love what your book looks like above anyone else, so design it how you want. Your unique way is the best way to go!

More Ideas for Editing

You can only do so much editing on the computer. After you've read your book several times on the computer, it can be easy to become familiar with it and look past mistakes without knowing it. And if you're like me, reading from the computer screen for so long can cause headaches.

So what are some other ways to edit without constantly having to look at a computer screen?

Well, letting someone else edit is helpful since it cuts down on the amount of editing you'll have to do all by yourself.

Print your book out! I know it takes a lot of ink and paper, but it's such a big help! You can then read your book on paper and mark edits, going back in later to fix errors. After you've printed your book, read over the paper pages several times as well. Use bright colored pens like red or orange to help you mark edits that need to be made later.

Read aloud! Reading your book aloud allows you to catch errors you may not have noticed by reading silently to yourself. Reading aloud with your editor can also be fun for both of you!

You got this, friend. Get in there, start reading, and edit to the end.

Publishing

Ever since I was a little girl, being published was always a distant dream in my imagination. It was never something I really saw as tangible, something that *I* could do. It was always something for those with more talent, more money, more experience.

I had those dreams running through my head of holding my very own book, signing my very own book, and flipping through the pages of my very own book.

I did so much researching on publishing when I was an early teenager and it only put a damper on my bright dreams.

Most of the publishing houses I checked out had major contracts involved, lots of money to be put up front, and rights to be signed over. Maybe I just never found the right publishing house for me, but none of these things were something that I wanted to do. Especially the cost. Way too much for a thirteen year old girl, who didn't even have a guarantee her books would sell!

And then somewhere along the way, the word *self-publishing* was presented to me.

I had no idea what it meant or what it would consist of, but the thought intrigued me. The idea that I could publish my own way was captivating to me. No need for fancy contracts or manuscript rejection letters.

Because here's the honest truth of what I believe.

I believe you have a story to share with the world.

If you've come this far, and you've written down the story—the words—that God has asked you to write, then it's time to publish them so the world can hear what He's given you to say.

You don't deserve rejection letters, because what you have to say is important. What you have to say might not be for everyone. You will have critics; that's just part of writing. What you have to say might not make everyone happy, but what you have to say is meant for *someone*. God didn't give you that book in your heart for it to stay in Microsoft Word where no one reads it.

And that's part of the beauty of self-publishing, because self-publishing gives you the freedom to share the words God has given at the time He calls you to. As soon as those words are written, edited, and formatted, they could be in the hands of a reader who desperately needs them.

Let me be clear though that I'm not against publishing houses, nor am I telling you to avoid them. If you want to publish with a major publishing house, go for it. Step into that adventure! It definitely also has its advantages and it's something I've considered for down the road as well. But for now, self-publishing is the best route for me. Choose the route that is best for *you*.

When I was going through the process of finding a self-publishing company, I looked up several options. I was surprised that the upfront cost of self-publishing was fairly low, and you retained all the rights to your work, something that meant a lot to me. You were the publisher, so *you* made all the decisions.

Then a friend told my sister and I about a company called CreateSpace.

Instead of discussing how CreateSpace works, it's easier just to direct you to their website at:

www.createspace.com

Before anything else, I strongly urge you to go check them out! They were the greatest, most helpful company I have worked with and it's been an honor to have them as a part of this journey. So please, if you want to go the self-published route, check out CreateSpace now! ☺

After you find the self-publishing company that you want to work with, that's only half the work.

With self-publishing, you are your own publisher. Which means all of the work falls on *your* shoulders. Self-publishing is not a "get rich quick" system, but it is the greatest thing God has ever allowed me to do. Publishing has never been about making a profit for me, but instead, all about letting the world hear the story God has placed in my heart.

With that being said, here are some quick things you'll have to remember if you chose to self-publish.

Cover Design

Cover design was one of the biggest obstacles for me because I had absolutely no idea how to do it! ☺ I knew exactly what I wanted my first book cover to look like, but I didn't know how to create that.

My sister directed me to a cover designer that she used for her debut novel, who was named Jasmine Ruigrok.

You can find Jasmine and her business, BushMaid Design & Lettering here on Facebook:
https://m.facebook.com/bushmaiddesign/

Or you can email Jasmine directly here: *bushmaid@gmail.com.*

Jasmine did an absolutely fantastic job with each one of my covers, far surpassing what I wanted. The price she charged me was affordable too, and I recommend her to any writer in need of a cover designer, especially if you're new to this thing.

If you're tech-savvy and would prefer to figure things out on your own instead, go for it! I've heard Microsoft Publisher works well for cover designing on your own, although I've never personally used it.

Honestly, the cover design part should be one of the most fun elements of publishing! You're finally bringing to life on a cover the words that have been in your heart for so long! Go for a cover that displays the heart of your book while displaying your personality at the same time.

Have fun!

Do it Afraid

I was finally there.

I had finally made it to the point where I could see the finish line of my writing and publishing journey. I was almost at the moment where I would hold my published book in my hands for the first time.

I had a release date set. It was coming up quickly.

And that was when I realized something.

I was terrified.

I was literally scared to death to publish my first book. I was agonizing over what I thought people would say, what their opinions would be. *Would people like my book? Would people disagree with me? Would my book be silly? Would my book make any difference at all?*

I was so scared I almost gave up. I was so close to backing out.

Because while writing is my deepest passion and joy, it also scares me to the core.

And sometimes I think that's the moment where you find your deepest calling.

That moment where your greatest joy and your greatest fear collide?

Yep, that's where your greatest calling is.

So this, my friend, is my message to you.

Do it afraid.

Approve that book to be published even if your hands are shaking while doing it.

The fear won't go away, so don't wait for it to. You can't waste your destiny away because of fear. It will always be there.

But here's the truth.

Bravery is taking the next step anyway, even when your legs are still shaking from fear.

You will face critics. Not everyone will love your book. You will have to deal with the naysayers.

That's part of the journey. You can't fear them forever.

So do it anyway, brave writer.

Do it afraid.

Sharing

You did it! You're finally here! You're at long last at the point in your journey where you get to share your work with the world. How exciting!

I am so thrilled for you getting to this point in your journey. Congratulations, from the bottom of my heart.

But now you may feel a little bit lost. Trust me, I felt a bit lost when *I Dare You* first released!

As a self-published author, the sole responsibility of marketing and sharing your book is entirely up to you. *You* are the one who has to get your name and your work out there. And at times that's not always easy. It can be hard to know how to go about letting others know that your book is published.

So in this section I want to give you tips on how to use every day social media that you likely are already using on a daily basis, to invite others into your writing journey. I'll also share some other fun ways you can spread the word.

Okay, ready?

Let's tell the world about your book!

Using Social Media

The world today is a fast-paced, social media focused culture. We are all about getting in touch faster and finding out the latest news as soon as it happens. If I had to guess, I'd say you probably use some form of social media at least once a day, even if it's just email. And come on, keeping a Snapchat streak is pretty fun too, right?

Well, below are some fun ways you can use social media to spread the word about your new book!

Facebook: More than likely, you probably have your own Facebook profile or you know someone who does. Use that to your advantage! Spread the word about your book and ask your friends to do the same to their friends! Take it a step further and set up your own author profile page. This was one of the first things I did when sharing about my book. By creating an author profile, I could invite my friends to like my page, thus spreading the word to lots of other people. Because my author page is public, anyone can see it, which also gives me lots more people I can reach.

Twitter: Who doesn't love creating a quirky, fun statement in 140 characters or less? ☺ This can be super fun to get the word going about your book! I have both a personal Twitter account and an account I use just for author things. Twitter is fun and easy because with just a quick click your followers can retweet your tweet, allowing their followers to see as well, and thus it keeps going! Something I like to do is take a short quote from my book and put it into a tweet, then tweet it for the world to see! This lets followers catch a glimpse of what your book is about.

Instagram: Okay, this is super fun and Instagram is probably my favorite! You can even go live on Instagram now to promote your book or do a Q&A for fun! Again I have a private Instagram account as well as a public one for my books and magazine. Post images or graphics with quotes from your book. A great app or website to use for this is Canva. I use them to design all of my blog and social media graphics! Follow people who follow similar interests or accounts that relate to your book in some way. You can use this for Twitter too. By doing this, you're letting these people find your account and learn about your book!

Google+: It took me until my third book before I finally started using Google+, but it can be super fun too. ☺ It can easily be used the way your other accounts are, and I find it more similar to Facebook. I know it can seem like a lot using all these different social media platforms but it's worth it in the end. By using most of the social media available to you, you can reach a broader audience. Maybe you'll reach someone on Google+ that you didn't reach on Twitter. So share, post, tweet, and snap! It'll be worth it!

Creating a Blog

I launched my blog that I titled *Worth it All,* on June 11, 2015.

I was beyond excited. I had dreamed of having a blog for years. My blog is one of my most special outlets for expressing my thoughts and lessons God teaches me that I want to share with my readers.

Not only is having a blog an incredible gift, but it can also be helpful in getting your writing out there which will help promote your book! Think about it. If readers have the opportunity to read what you have to say for free online, they will be more likely to spend money buying your book because they already know they like your writing.

You can use your blog to post updates about when your book is releasing or you can even use it to post excerpts from your book! I've used it for both! I've used my blog to have blog parties to celebrate the release of my last two books as well.

One thing I want to advise is to not use your blog as a place to share anything and everything about your life. A blog is still public and on the internet for anyone to see. Use your discretion with what you share. Don't be afraid to share your heart about a subject, but just be careful the amount of personal details you share.

If you'd like to check out my blog to see what kind of posts I started with and what kind of posts I still write, feel free to check it out:

www.Jesusisworthitall.weebly.com

Creating a Website

Another super fun adventure is creating a website! ☺

If you already have a blog, you may choose to skip this step. I have both a website and a blog and I use Weebly for them both.

One thing to keep in mind when creating a website is to have fun with it, just like anything else! Let your website reflect your book. Try to use the same color schemes as your book if you want, and similar fonts or designs to make everything flow well. Or if you're like me and prefer to mix things up, go for that too. ☺

On your website list the places where your book can be purchased and also include a contact form where readers can contact you directly.

Share about your book and give your own bio as well, including your writing background. Again, because a website is public on the internet, always be careful what details you include in a bio. If you don't want the whole world knowing something, don't share it.

Giveaways

Yay! I love this part! Probably because I'm just happy for people to have my books, I'd much rather give them away than sell them. ☺

Doing giveaways is a super fun way to raise your reader audience too! If someone wins a copy of your book and enjoys it, they have more reason to either buy a copy then for a friend or buy your next book!

The thing I love about giveaways is that this part isn't so much about making money as it is about letting someone into your journey. When someone reads your book, they are walking a piece of your journey with you. I love this opportunity to let people step in and walk a bit of the path with me.

There are fun ways you can do giveaways too! Use social media to your advantage. For example, on Twitter, let your followers know that the first fifteen people to retweet you will get entered into a giveaway for a copy of your book! Use this on other social media too! By having those who enter like, share, or retweet your post, they're helping you spread the word about your book while getting something out of it themselves!

Book Signings

I did my first book signing shortly after *I Dare You* released. My mom did the majority of the work for this signing and I'm so thankful to her for that.

Book signings are meant to be welcoming and inviting, so create a fun atmosphere! We put out yummy cookies (no, I promise I didn't eat *all* of them), and sodas.

When having a book signing, do something to draw in attendance. Perhaps do a live book reading where you read a chapter from your book. Play a game related to your book. Have an author Q&A. If you've written a fiction book, get some friends to help you act out a short skit from one of your scenes.

And yes, free food is always helpful too. ☺

Your display is everything, so design your table to look epic! Use things that bring out what your book is about!

For my display, I had my book sitting up with several candles around it, since a candle is the main theme of my cover. I also included cards on the table that shared little encouragement from each chapter of my book!

My twin sister had her book signing for her novel *Not Abandoned* at the same time as me, and her display was amazing too! Because her book deals with human trafficking, she had a chain wrapped around the bottom of the stand her book was sitting in. She also created character sheets with pictures of what she wanted her characters to look like and little facts about them.

Local libraries would probably be more than willing to allow you, a local author, to have your book signing at the library.

That's where I did mine. If not, check with your church! They might allow you to have your book signing there. Or check out a local community center or bookstore.

A quick tip is to let your local newspaper know about your book and your book signing! This will give you lots of free publicity that is super helpful. I had two or three local newspapers interview me and talk about my book signing. A young, local author is big news people will want to read about so let your newspaper or local TV station know. Who knows, maybe you'll get your local TV station to show up at your book signing to do a feature on you!

Story Prompts

In this section we're going to have some fun! This part is specifically for all the fiction writers out there! And if you've never written fiction before, give it a try! You might surprise yourself at how much fun you have. ☺

We all know it's a lot easier to write a story or a book if we have inspiration for it or if we've been given a prompt to go off of. Even just a sentence of a few words can spark ideas that weren't previously flowing.

So because of that, this section is filled with just a few story prompts to get your ideas going and your fingers typing! Are you ready?

Let's have some fun!

Sentence Prompts:

- Every life leaves a mark on the lives around them. Make the mark count.
- Flowers emerging from the dirt remind us that life can begin again, even after we think it's over.
- Hope keeps holding on when everything else says to let go.
- Never forget who you are now, especially when being reminded of who you once were.
- Seasons change, just like our lives.
- Faith keeps believing when everything else says it's impossible.
- Memories help to remind us of where we have been. But we sometimes cannot let them keep us from where we are going.
- The heroes are the ones who do the courageous thing, even when the risk is great.

- Tell the story of a betrayal and a crazy act of forgiveness.
- Never forget His faithfulness in your life story.
- Sometimes things don't always go as planned, and that's where plan B comes in.

Question Prompts:

- What would happen if your character's least favorite job suddenly became their passion?
- What would happen if your character's past comes back to them in a new, difficult way?
- What would happen if your character's best friend goes missing?
- If your character was trapped in an abandoned building and only had twenty-six minutes to figure a way out, what would they do?
- If your character had to board a public plane without other passengers recognizing them,

what would be their go-to disguise?

➤ What would happen if your famous character's true identity suddenly came to light?

➤ What would happen if your character met someone in a park who would change their life? Who is this person?

➤ If your character were faced with a life threatening situation, who would be the first person they would call?

➤ Why does your character always go to the downtown bowling alley at midnight? Who are they meeting?

➤ Who is your character most afraid of meeting again?

Funny Prompts:

➤ Tell the story of a crazy day at the park and a runaway pet mouse.

- You overflow the washing machine on your first day working at the palace.
- Tell the story of two best friends who lose an important piece of information in a foreign country, and their plan to retrace their steps until they find it again.
- Tell the story of a day gone badly for the new zookeeper at the local zoo.
- Tell the story of a circus—from a lazy tiger's point of view!

Writing Exercises

This is just a fun, little section where you can sharpen your writing skills and get more experience! ☺ I've come up with these exercises from over ten years of writing experience and these are things that have worked to help me. Everyone is different so these may or may not be helpful to you to give inspiration or get the writing flowing. Feel free to switch things up, or to do your own thing. Writing is all about originality and being yourself, so fix these exercises to suite you. Also, there are dozens of books out there to help with writing exercises, so you should totally check some out at the library too. And there's Pinterest for those tech people out there! ☺

Okay, let's go!

Writing Exercise #1:

Sit down with a pen and paper and take the next ten minutes to write out a narrative about your day. You could use a personal journal or just a random piece of paper. Just make sure you are using a pen and paper and not a computer keyboard! Write about a certain event, or share the details of one moment, or just quickly jot down what happened that day. This is simply an exercise to get words flowing and get you writing *something*.

Writing Exercise #2:

Find your favorite writing partner and challenge each other to thirty minutes of writing a random short story. Maybe you'll want to use one of the prompts from the last section! See who can write the most words (and the best story!) in those thirty minutes. Have a third person judge the stories if you're up for that. A little competition is always good for the soul and is definitely fun! ☺

Writing Exercise #3:

Create a list of names. This is actually super fun! But, no, google is not acceptable. These must be original names you come up with, think of, or create on your own. Create a boy name list, a girl name list, and even a last name list if you're up for a challenge! Sometimes the foundation of a great novel is the perfect main character name. Use these to create perfect names for your characters.

Writing Exercise #4:

Create character profiles. This allows you to form a character that is real to you. List their favorite color, their favorite TV show, what they do when they're sad, random facts about them—list it all! Create someone real that your readers will be able to connect with. Having a foundation of who your character is, also helps you as you begin writing. Don't forget that when writing, allow your character to have some mystery in the beginning! Let them evolve throughout the novel. Don't tell everything about them or even their history in the first chapter.

Writing Exercise #5:

Go find some of your stories or articles from a couple years ago, whether they were written on a computer or in notebooks. If you're new to writing and don't have any older works, just pick out your first few articles/stories. We can all learn from our experience, so take about twenty-thirty minutes just to focus on improving your older stories with what you've learned from the experience of writing. Edit and develop your story better. Always save your original copy though! Those are always fun to look back on several years down the road. ☺

Writing Exercise #6:

Write aloud! Every word you type, speak it out loud. This will not only allow you to slow down and process what you're writing better, but it gives you an idea of how it's going to sound to a reader. Speak out loud whatever you type.

Writing Exercise #7:

Write your story into a poem! This may seem like a weird concept but it can be fun, and help to develop the purpose of your story better in your mind. Whatever the plot of your story is, or the theme of it is, write it into a poem. It doesn't have to be long, a few phrases is sufficient. Just make sure you get your point of the story across in the poem!

Writing Exercise #8:

Write an essay of *why* you write. Share your heart. Explain exactly *why* you choose to put your words onto paper. Do you just like using writing as a pastime? Do you write to let your voice be heard? Do you write to say what you can't say with your lips? Do you write to have fun? Do you write to inspire others? Do you write to invite others into your make-believe world? Whatever your reason, share it in an essay!

Writing Exercise #9:

Create a writing playlist! I work best with music and every single one of my books has been written while listening to music. I usually create special playlists for my books, but sometimes I just shuffle through all of my music. Create your own playlist of music that matches the tone and style of your book and use it to create inspiration as you write.

Writing Exercise #10:

Take a story from your life and write it as a fictional tale! Rename all of the characters, even yourself! Maybe you can tell the story of you and your best friend's craziest adventure together. Maybe you can write about a concert that changed your life. Or maybe you can write about a trip to the zoo. Just have fun re-creating one of your favorite memories.

A Word about Dreams

You know that dream in your heart that not many people know about?

That dream you hold close but are afraid it will never come true?

That dream God handed you but you aren't sure what to do with it?

Don't *ever, ever* give up on that dream.

Dreams are a funny thing. They can consume every part of our lives and completely change us inside and out, yet it's so easy to just keep them to ourselves.

Because the truth?

We're scared.

Our dreams scare us.

So many times it can be easy to think that our dreams are beyond our grasp because they may be too impossible or unachievable. Because of this it becomes easy to give up on our dreams and live a "normal" life that is all about climbing the corporate ladder and having all the latest fashion trends, obeying what the world tells you to do.

But what happened to that once innocent, child-like faith you held in your heart when you were younger, and you closed your eyes and dared to dream? When did you let it go? *When did you lose it?*

Today I can search my name on Amazon and it brings up three book titles.

Today I can hold three books in my hands with the author name being "*Isabella D. Morganthal.*" Today I can work on my monthly e-magazine that almost 100 girls receive. Today I can write on my blog and share my thoughts with a world that I hope to inspire with truth. And because of that, tonight I am here to tell you....*dreams come true when God is in the center.*

I'm here to tell you I've dreamed about this moment for ten years, over half my life. Being an author was my life dream. Writing a blog was something I've dreamed of since my early teen years. Sharing my writing with the world is what makes my heart come alive.

And if you would've told me ten years ago I'd be here today, the author of three books, the editor and founder of my own e-magazine, and a blogger, I never would've believed you.

But here I am.

And it's all because of *Him.*

So let me tell you, when God is in the center of your dreams, He gives them back to you in a more beautiful way than you ever thought possible. He makes them amazing, because He gave them to you to start with. He will take you on an adventure that will be beyond your wildest imagination.

So that dream in your heart? Hold onto it and pursue it, won't you?

Never give up on your dreams, dear one.

Place them in His hands.

It will be incredible. I promise.

To God be the glory!

"Not unto us, O Lord, not unto us, but to Your Name give glory, because of Your mercy, because of Your truth."

~Psalm 115:1~

Thank You...

To the people who have inspired, challenged, influenced, and changed my life in more ways than one. To the people who have walked beside me on my writing journey and supported me every step of the way. **Thank you...**

Mom, Dad, Kenzie, Brandon, Rachel, Bethany, Courtney, Dani, Lindsay, Grace, Beth, Megan, Olivia, Heidi, Corey, Livy, Kylie, Christine, Abby, Ryan, *The King's Princess* magazine subscribers, *Worth it All* blog followers, Brittany, Tiffany, Sarah, CreateSpace team, Ann Voskamp, Holley Gerth, Jen Ledger, John and Korey Cooper, Seth Morrison, Katie Davis, Lacey Sturm, my faithful readers.

To you.
Thank you for entering a piece of my journey.

Contact

I would love to hear from you! Whether you've got questions, concerns, thoughts, or comments, I'd love to get connected with you! As family in Christ we are meant to support and encourage one another. I'd love to do that for you in your writing journey. So if you want to get connected with me here is how:

Email:
thekingsprincessmagazine@gmail.com
Website:
www.isabellamorganthal.weebly.com
Blog: www.Jesusisworthitall.weebly.com
Magazine Website:
www.thekingsprincessmagazine.weebly.com
Twitter: @authorbella2015
Facebook: @isabellamorganthal
Instagram: @thekingsprincessmagazine

*Let's talk soon, friend!
Keep writing!* ♥

~Other Books from this Author~

I Dare You: *Finding Your Passion and Lighting Your World*

The King's Princess: *A Magazine Compilation*

Worth it All: *Running the Race of a Lifetime*

Made in the USA
Columbia, SC
07 May 2017